Unlock your potential in the workplace - Volume 2 – Be a Leader not a Boss by Daniel Dias

Published by Amazon

www.uyourp.com

© 2020 Daniel Dias

All rights reserved. No portion of this book may be reproduced in any form without permission from the publisher, except as permitted by U.S. copyright law. For permissions contact:

uyourp@gmail.com

ISBN: 9798665369426

ABOUT MYSELF 5

CHAPTER 1   THE TEAM 9

   INTRODUCTION 11
   BUILD THE PERFECT TEAM 13
   KNOW YOUR EMPLOYEES 15
   KNOW YOUR TEAM 21
   2ND IN COMMAND 47

CHAPTER 2   ENGAGEMENT 53

   INTRODUCTION 55
   GOOD WORK CONDITIONS 57
   THEIR WORK MATTERS 60
   CLEAR CAREER PATH 62
   EMPOWER YOUR EMPLOYEES 64
   HAVE ONE TO ONE TALKS 68
   BUSINESS TRIPS 76
   RECOGNITION WHO, WHEN, HOW 78

CHAPTER 3   MINORITIES 83

   INTRODUCTION 85
   DIVERSITY 86
   EMPLOYEE RESOURCE GROUP 91
   SPONSORED EMPLOYEES 94

CHAPTER 4   TEAM MANAGEMENT 97

   INTRODUCTION 99
   COMPANY POLICY & PROCESSES 100
   FLEXIBLE TIME 108
   CHANGE 113
   STRATEGIC THINKING 122
   WAR BOARD 127
   MERITS 132
   BUILD BRIDGES 135
   SURVEYS 138

CHAPTER 6   DISCIPLINARY ACTIONS 141

   INTRODUCTION 143

PERFORMANCE IMPROVEMENT PLAN (PIP) 144
LAYOFFS 151
WRAPPING UP 156

ABOUT MYSELF

If you had a chance to read volume 1 – Emotional Intelligence & job interviews, you already know a little about me, but in case you missed it, let me introduce myself.

I am an Engineer Manager with more than 15 years' experience in the Automotive and Aerospace industries. Worked and lived in multiple countries. I also possess several management degrees that allow me to be a better leader, better professional, and person.

My passion is to lead multicultural teams to achieve success. I can tell you there is usually a better, smarter way to do things, to be assertive and go beyond your expectations if you believe in yourself, trust your instincts, let go of the fear of failure, be open to learning new things, and don't let others push you back.

I will share the knowledge and tools I used by working in several countries and corporations as an engineer and manager. I intend to be as forthcoming as possible, crude, to say things as they really are and how they worked for me. I gathered valuable information from my experience and from research to lay it here down for you in a simple, down to earth manner. You will be able to apply it starting day one. I worked with all kinds of people in different positions in a company, from the shop floor to CEOs/Company owners, with different cultures, from different countries and different generations. I failed as much as I succeeded.

I made mistakes, made breakthroughs, embraced both, and learned with both. I am here to help you. My goal is to empower you to have a new perspective, become smarter, see the signs in front of you, and grab the opportunities. I had some help during my work life, and now that I am in my 40s, I decided it is time to share my knowledge with others.

Continuing to evolve in my career, always learning and open to new experiences and challenges. Workplaces are complex and in movement, not static places where one rule applies to all. Come and learn how to navigate through rough water to get to your desired goal.

Remember, never stop trying. Move forward for what you believe, for what you want. Don't be afraid of making mistakes or getting hurt in the process. The wounds heal with time, but the opportunities, if you don't grab them, they tend to disappear.

My goal with this book is to help you become a better leader, a real leader, someone whose team members can look at with admiration. Someone they feel they can trust no matter what adversities, who is on the same boat with them, roaming together in the same direction towards success.

In this book, I am going to focus only on corporate professionals. What I am going to mention here can be used in other kinds of teams, but my experience is on corporate companies and especially in Engineer professionals.

Chapter 1
THE TEAM

INTRODUCTION

What is a team? What defines a team? Why do we even need to have teams in the workplace working for the same goal? And Why is a manager necessary to get a team to roam the boat in the same direction?

I met managers that think and act like a team is just a group of professionals in the same place with the same objective that you just need to give instructions or assign a goal for the job to appear done on time and with quality. Others think a team to work together needs to be micromanaged. You need to be on top of them every minute, push them, and tell them what to do from the beginning to the end.

What differentiates people and the way they are in society and the workplace? First genetics, right? A genetic mix has a part in defining who we are. We also have the way we were raised, the culture we belong, our religion, our experiences growing up, the country we were born, and many other things. We are not clones of each other, and we are all different. We have entirely different hobbies, different things we like to do, different things we love doing for fun or work. Some of us wake up earlier in the morning and are very optimistic. Others don't like that at all and are pessimists, always seeing the negative side of life.

Some of us have prominent families, and others do not. Some have family problems, health problems, debts, etc.

Where I am trying to get is we all become very different, and deal with situations like stress and schedules very differently.

How do you get all these kinds of professionals to be on the same boat and take direction from you? Understand your instructions and roam in the same direction, motivated, pushing hard, and feel fulfilled in the end?

BUILD THE PERFECT TEAM

Figure 1 - Photo courtesy of rawpixel.com

Is not very often you can build your team from scratch. If that is your case, then you should probably prepare yourself how to choose the best candidates and excel in your job interview skills. I am not going to talk about those cases in this book because I already do in the book "Unlock your potential in the workplace – Volume 1 - Emotional intelligence & job interviews".

If you have the chance to build your great team, don't lose the opportunity to have a great team because you are not prepared to grab the best candidates. Creating your team is a chance for you to have the perfect group but also a greater responsibility to your management.

In most cases, you inherit an existing team, and you have to do your best to know them and make them work together as a team.

Having already a team does not mean you are stuck with it for life. If someone is not performing, it can be layoff or send to another department, and you can fill the opening with a more suitable employee. Layoffs are the last thing you want to do. It impacts an employee's life. It costs money to the company and will influence others morally.

There is a lot you can do before firing someone as you can find one this book, from training, PIP – Performance improvement plan, and other methods, tools.

Let me show you ways to empower you as a leader, unite your team and make them one force like a group of pistons in a combustion engine.

KNOW YOUR EMPLOYEES

Figure 2 - Photo courtesy of rawpixel.com

I have managed many teams, international teams, different generations, and races. Do you think people working together as a team has to like each other? Many think so. I don't.

What I learned all these years leading teams is, for a team to work, they have to respect and trust each other and their manager. They need to feel they all are part of the team. If one fails, all fail if one wins all win. I remember in one of my jobs as an engineer working with the shop floor to get a prototype built, and I never forget the advice from the production manager.

I treated shop floor people with respect and was very polite, and in return, they would help me a lot and engage in conversations that create bonds of trust. There are always those who try to take advantage of you being friendly and respectful to start disrespectfully treating you and abuse your trust. Those usually are not the majority, and you can make sure you are respected, as I will show you further in this book.

I am getting ahead, so let's go back to the advice from the production manager. His advice was for me to be ruff and treat people like I am the boss looking upon them, to give orders, and talk rudely. If I didn't do that, they would take advantage of me and not respect me. He was not able to manage his team correctly. He was not their leader. He was a boss, a dictator, giving blunt orders that had to be followed without question. He disregarded their experience of many years on the job and the valuable input they could offer.

So how do you know your team? You can manage a team for five years and don't know your team. The professionals on your team are not just the work they do. They have families, personal problems, hobbies, like sports, travel, etc. What I mean is get to know your team, what makes them move, tick.

Many years ago, I met a site director that every day would go to the shop floor and talk with people and knew everyone by name. They had more than 100 people on the shop floor, and he treated them like family, so much than when the company was going through a rough time and was about to close because of the global financial crisis, all employees worked for free for more than three months and saved the company. You can say they did it to keep their jobs, but everyone said that they did it and refused other jobs because of the director.

Every morning when you get to work and leave at the end of the day, compliment your employees with a good morning or see you tomorrow. During the day, take 1 hour to visit each one and ask how everything is going, in work and family, just have a chat and get to know them, this will create a bond and trust.

Many managers avoid this because they find it difficult to discipline or lay off employees that you get to know better. Well, that's part of your job, you should be able to do one thing without compromising the other.

One thing worse than don't get to know your team is if you try to get to know them, engage them in conversations, and you sound fake, don't mean what you say and don't give the proper attention. Be truthful, go as far you feel comfortable, and also as far the employee feels comfortable, don't push for details, just have a coffee break conversation.

If any of your employees comes to you to talk about personal or professional issues, let go of your computer, ask him or her to sit down and give the proper attention. You probably think that you are too busy and do not have time for that. Take the time to do it, it will pay off, and if you don't do it, you will lose much more time trying to get things on time with employees that are not motivated and fill no one cares about them.

We all have urgent things to do, and if you have to finish an email or have an urgent meeting or anything else, just say to the employee that you have to do something urgently and will come back to him or her. So after you finish your urgent task, call the employee to your office, don't forget to do that.

I am a very private person, I don't share personal information easily, and I respect the privacy of others very much, so be curious, show interest but avoid being noisy. Only talk about something that was brought in conversation by the employee. For example, if an employee asks to leave earlier because a family member is sick, the next day asks how that family member is doing.

Don't forget, always follow up something an employee told you or asked you.

It is not difficult to do, and this will go a long way. It will help you achieve your milestones. It will motivate the team and help them engaged because if you care about them, they will care about you and the company.

Don't wait, don't hesitate. If you have the same team for some time and this is the first time you will try to get to know your team members better, you will see from your employees some reactions of suspicion or particular odd looks. Probably they are thinking about what the catch is or what is going on. Just keep doing it until it becomes a routine. I had employees asking me directly why the change of behavior and if that happens, be honest, not too honest, just say you should have done that from the beginning, you were not able before but from now on you are.

I know my team, I know it very well, they are very open with me. I try to help my team members and listen to them as much as possible.

Remember the saying and incite it to your team:

"A single twig breaks, but the bundle of twigs is strong."

Tecumseh

KNOW YOUR TEAM

Figure 3 - Photo courtesy of rawpixel.com

One thing is to know your team members. Another thing is to know your team, see how they interact with each other, and make them work as one. A group of people needs guidance from an excellent leader to function correctly and smoothly.

As an example, think of a choir or an orchestra. You can have ten people that sing or play an instrument beautifully by themselves, but to make them all sing or play as one is another different thing. A team at work is the same thing. To make it work as a team, it requires dedication, training, tact, empathy, and time. Especially in the beginning, you need to dedicate a lot of your time to make them work as one. After you get some inertia, you can relax your interaction with your team and just maintain the energy going.

How do you start evaluating your team? The first thing to do is to listen and observe. Keep your eyes and ears open. In the next paragraph, you could find what I observed and did to improve team interactions and health in the first stages.

EMPLOYEES WHO HAVE ALWAYS NEGATIVE COMMENTS ABOUT THE COMPANY, THE JOB OR THE PROCESSES. EVERYTHING IS IMPOSSIBLE TO ACHIEVE

Figure 4 - Photo courtesy of pixabay

These types of employees have a dramatic impact on your team dynamics, productivity, and this should be handled quickly. Negativism can spread like cancer. It will spread to your team, and it will reach the rest of the company. I have seen the performance of teams go down as much as 50% just because of one employee.

So what can you do if you have one of these professionals in your team? Most of the time, you cannot just layoff, and

I believe you should always try to speak with the employee first. I can tell you the rate of success to have one of these employees to change his or her ways is low. They will stop for a while or will just continue doing outside the office or on the coffee break.

Like I first mentioned, what you need to do is to call the negative employee to your office and let him or her know that his or her behavior is not acceptable and that he or she is influencing the team negatively. Explain the consequences for him or her if the behavior does not change. Also, mention the effects on the team and the company in general. Try to know if he or she is unhappy with their current job and if there is a place in the company that they would be happy doing.

Yes, to the business. One person's negativity can make you lose employees, customers, and decrease the quality of your products.

Observe the employee. Look at his or her body language if there is negativity in the way they act, stand, cross arms, always frown or fuming. Just be vigilant.
If the behavior returns, you don't have any other choice then to raise a PIP – Performance Improvement Plan to

more directly show the employee his or her behavior needs to improve.

I will talk about PIP in chapter 6.

EMPLOYEES WHO ARE ALWAYS READY TO HELP

Figure 5 - Photo courtesy of Visual Tag MX

These are precious team members who take the initiative to help colleagues. Praise him or her, and when they get the necessary experience, make them leads.

Just make sure he or she does not help too much and miss his or her deadlines.

You shouldn't micromanage the employee but instead, explain that he or she is free to help, but they still have to meet their objectives, and it is his or her responsibility to manage their time.

EMPLOYEES WHO ARE ALWAYS ASKING FOR HELP TO THEIR COLLEAGUES

Figure 6 - Photo courtesy of Lukas

It is normal when you have a new employee, new to the business, to ask regularly for help to their colleagues until he or she gets to speed. What is not normal is a professional that works for, let's say a year, and still "harasses" colleagues regularly to help on things they should have picked up a long time ago.

This behavior is not suitable for team harmony. It will make mad some team members for being always bothered and stressed because then they have to catch up with the time they lost helping. The worst type is even that employee that asks you for help, not coming to your desk but asking you to go to his or her desk instead.

I had more than once this kind of team members, and they have this behavior for 3 reasons:

Lack of training

Some team members have this behavior because they lack the training. It is not unusual for an employee to have a lack of training and don't communicate with his or her supervisor. Many are afraid to show they lack specific knowledge and prefer to get the instruction on the day to day basis from colleagues.

It is your job as a team manager to make sure people feel safe and at ease reaching out to you, saying they are struggling in a particular area, and it is your job to make sure they have the training they need. They can even be trained by colleagues but in a planned way and not a day to day routine of interrupting colleagues.

Some are afraid to mention they lack the knowledge because they actually don't have it, and on the job interview, they had to be on this job said they did. Usually, the company gives a candidate three months on a trial basis. Use these three months wisely to evaluate the employee.

Lack of skills

You must be thinking; if they have a lack of skills, then they need training. You are correct, but what I mean here with a lack of skills is when you have someone who does not have in them what is required to do what is expected of them for that job.

Even if you train them, push them, they will probably improve a little but will come right back to the same again. You only have three options here. One, you move that person to another department where he or she can be more productive or two, you give him or her more manageable tasks or three, you need to let the employee go. It is that simple.

I had two employees like this on my team. Usually, they are older and cannot keep up with technological advances. I was able to move one to another department where he could keep up easily. He, at one time, thanked me for the change. He was happier and more relaxed. The other, I start giving him simpler projects that the company always has, and he was doing fine also.

Remember we are dealing with people and I have a lot of respect for older people in the company. Lay off an employee should always be, always the last resource when all the other options were exhausted.

Lack of interest - laziness

Investigate the lack of interest first. Try to find out if the employee was always like that. Investigate if there was a certain point there was a change. Talk to the employee. Tell him or her your concerns and the impact of his or her behavior on the team. Inform as well, what are going to be the consequences if he or she continues to act like that.

Consequences usually are disciplinary. Typically, the employee will go through a PIP – Performance Improvement Plan, and second, if the pip goes down the drain, it has to be laid off.

EMPLOYEES WHO SAY IMPROPER THINGS TO OR ABOUT COLLEAGUES

Figure 7 - Photo courtesy of Gratisography

In most companies, there are strict policies to be followed: no harassment, no discrimination, threats, and other kinds of disrespectful, aggressive or bullying behavior.
Anything even related to this is unacceptable also if it is considered a joke.

There are 2 cases I remember clearly. The first was related to employees that frequently talked about politics and were very disrespectful with others that opposed their opinions. The arguments sometimes would escalate to unacceptable levels.

The employees were warned once about their behavior and a disciplinary action open. The behavior stopped. If it didn't, the next option could be to suspend the employees without pay and, in worst cases, action to layoff the involved employees.

Another employee I had used to joke a lot with colleagues, but sometimes it would get out of hand. One time he said to another employee that he needed his help right away, and if the response would be "not possible right now", he made some kind of joke that he had a gun in the car.

The offended made a complaint against him to HR that open a disciplinary action. He apologized, and it never happened again.

It does not matter what the intention was. These behaviors are unacceptable and have to be dealt with promptly. If the situation is not handled immediately, harmony will end in the office. People will leave, and the company will go down.

EMPLOYEES WHO TALK BAD ABOUT THEIR COLLEAGUES TO THEIR MANAGER

Figure 8 - Photo courtesy of Tirachard Kumtanom

You should always encourage your team to talk with you, to feel free to enter your office if they have a concern or question, well, for anything. It is ok when an employee comes to you to talk about a colleague that he or she has a concern, for example, if they are getting late on their commitment to close a task because another colleague is late and he or she needs his or her input.

It's ok to mention that he or she is always late, and it is not the first time his or her job is impacted. That is the limit in this example if it goes any further, for example, the employee starting to mention that he or she does not belong to the team, no one likes him or her, does not watch his or her hands, and others, I heard them all.

Sometimes there are exceptions. One time I had an employee come to me very nervous and told me that if he could change desks because for a week now his colleague really smelled and he cannot take it anymore.

I told him I had a look at it and went to that employee to talk about work and could "smell" that the complaint was legit.

After talking with the employee who smelled, I found out he was going through a very rough phase in his life. He was divorcing, and his kids were moving to another state. He lost his house and was living in a new place but had no water yet. I asked him if he could take a bath in the bathrooms we had for the shop floor employees. He told me he would feel ashamed if someone sees him, and I arranged a way for him to get in sooner when no one was on the company yet. When I got home that day, I bought him some shampoo, bath gel, razor, shaving cream, and other things and left it on the bathroom for him.

The next day he comes crying to my office thanking me for everything.

You never know what is happening in an employee's life, so always be assertive, empathic, and don't jump to conclusions.

EMPLOYEES WHO DON'T INTERACT WITH OTHERS

Figure 9 - Photo courtesy of Djordje Petrovic

We don't have to be all the same, act the same way. No, of course not, but if you have one of your team members that do not interact at all with the other team members or with the manager and lacks giving valuable information, the status of a specific work, that's a problem.

As a team, they have to work together at least at some point and need to give you feedback promptly, especially if the schedule is compromised. Smart introverted people should have technical jobs, something they could do by themselves.

EMPLOYEES WHO SPEND MORE TIME TALKING WITH COLLEAGUES OR ON THE PHONE AND INTERNET THAN WORKING

Figure 10 - Photo courtesy of rawpixel.com

I am all forward for my employees to talk between themselves about day to day things. I believe it is healthy and unites the team in such a way that you, as their manager, you should even encourage them.

I am also ok for my employees to check sometimes the internet or phones for personal matters. It helps them relax and decompress.

What is not ok, is when an employee tells me he is going to miss a goal. He or she gives me an invented excuse or insinuates that the scope was more significant than expected when I know the same employee lost a lot of time on personal business, one the phone, internet, or just talking all day.

I had an employee that had in one of his screens the stock market live. He would do this every day. I believe it was a way to be able to make some extra money to support his big family.

This behavior is not acceptable. The company is not paying you to play in the stock market. After I warned the employee, I never saw his screen again with the stock market. After a few weeks, I start seeing him always looking at his table. I found out that he was looking still at the stock market on his phone now. To make things worse, he ever had an excuse to be late.

One of my employees likes to talk a lot with the other colleagues, a little too much. She would do it all day every day. She would meet her dates, but she was making other colleagues late. I am not here to babysit anyone. Every employee should be responsible for managing their time and avoid the conversation if he or she has work to do. In this case, I open an exception since it was over the charts.

I just called her to my office and explained the situation. She significantly reduced the chatting, affirming she never noticed she was talking that much.

One thing that you should have in mind is if you have an employee that always meets his or her goals and spends a lot of time doing other things than work, then you probably need to plan better the workload for that employee. The company pays the employees to do work for the company.

EMPLOYEES WHO HAVE GREAT IDEAS THAT HELP IMPROVE PROCESSES, ARE ALWAYS READY TO DO EXTRA TIME IF ANYTHING URGENT COMES UP

Figure 11 - Photo courtesy of Pixabay

Keep these employees in your team at all costs. Give them challenging assignments, responsibilities, more power, and responsibilities. Prepare them to lead a team one day.

Be their mentor, train them, and learn to trust them to do their thing their way. Always keep the trust and communication lines open. Have a clear career path and expectations. They can feel they have input and control, but don't try to have them under your control or manipulate things to have them stay on your team, and they will sense it and jump out of the boat quickly.

You, as a manager, will thrive with this kind of employee, of course. Their success is your success. I knew managers that took advantage of their best employees to boost their careers and never compensate the people on their teams. No raises, no bonus, and sometimes even a thank you. You can advance your career using others, but one day you will pay the price for that. I believe in karma and that for every action, there is a reaction, a consequence.

I don't just believe it. I have seen it hundreds of times. It happens quickly for some and others after many years but always happens. Treat your team with respect, work with them for them, not only for you, and you will be respected and admired by them and the company.

EMPLOYEES WHO WANT OTHERS TO SLOW DOWN

Figure 12 - Photo courtesy of Frans Van Heerden

There are faster employees than others, and that is normal. After you know all your team members well, you can quickly predict who will be able to do a specific task in a certain time frame. You need to plan around it and not to put everything on your best team members.

When I started as an engineer on my first aerospace company, I was excited and did things fast and had a lot of creative ideas and I remember listening more than once someone from my team saying for me to slow down, not to go so fast because then they will look bad. I never slowed down, and you should also do not allow anyone to say that to your team members. Many times people say that because they are afraid, afraid to lose their jobs, afraid they are not seen anymore as the source to get things done. Talk with the employee that is trying to slow others down, explain that you understand not all run the same speed, and that is OK. Don't forget to mention how they are valuable to the team.

EMPLOYEES WHO ARE ALWAYS LATE AND MISSES IMPORTANT MEETINGS

Figure 13 - Photo courtesy of rawpixel.com

You should always get on time for your appointments and meetings. There are, of course, things that you cannot predict like a road accident or a flat but in general, you should arrive on time.

Whenever you are late for a meeting, you are disrespectful to the person that schedules the meeting and everyone else present.

If you have an employee that is always late, don't jump into conclusions and go to speak with him or her. Explain that because he or she is delayed, it creates a bad precedent, impacts the entire team schedule and your own.

Let me tell you about my experience. I had an employee that was always punctual, never missed a meeting, and one day she started to get in late, missing the first-morning meeting. She was a good, reliable team member, so I did not say anything until this was going on for a week.

I called her to my office, and I asked her why the change of behavior. She put her head down and was reluctant to talk. I told her everything that she would say to me is confidential and would not get out of the office unless she was ok with it. She told me she had financial problems and her car needed repair, but did not have the money for it so she would take the bus or walk to work every day. She tried to wake up earlier, but she is so tired from the previous day that is difficult for her to do it.

I asked if I get somehow for her a ride with another colleague from the same area if that would work?
She said yes, and I was able to get her a ride until she could get the car fixed. One of the company members lived just a block away.

After that successful story, the company created a car share program for people to share the car, gas costs, and at the same time, help the planet, and it was a success.

There are many other types of employees that I did not mention here probably, but these are probably the most common cases that I think you can relate to.

Remember, every person is different, so act accordingly and try to make your team-work as one.

EMPLOYEE WHO IS FAST AND KNOWLEDGEABLE

Figure 14 - Photo courtesy of Startup stock photos

Usually, you have a top performer on your team, the one who does things in half the time and with better quality. I have the luck to have 3 of those in my group out of 10, and one thing that I try to avoid is to overload them with work just because they can do it better or faster.

It is tempting to assign the more difficult task to them all the time and ask them to stop what they are doing and help in other urgent issues that pop up. One of the leader's tasks is to assign work to the team members, and after a while, they know what kind of jobs they will perform better than others.

I try to have a balance. If, because of schedule, I have no option but to assign more difficult tasks to my best employees, ask more time and commitment out of them, and I do it more than one time in a row, I have to someone award them. I will always talk with them and tell them how good they did and what was the impact on the company that quarter and that the company is aware of their excellent work, but I also go the extra mile or to give them an increase or a spot award for their efforts.

If I have time, if schedule permits, even knowing they I could improve dates using my best again, I sometimes give them slack, give them easy tasks and let the other to the more difficult tasks. On the other hand, since now they are going to have extra time, they will help the others, train them, and check their work when it is finished. So I am using them to teach the others, and at the same time, I am uniting the team and make them work better together.

If you put all the weight in your rock star employee, and especially if you don't recognize his or her work, he or she will eventually quit, and your team will be in a much worst place.

2nd IN COMMAND

Figure 15 - Photo courtesy of Rebrand Cities

You need to choose one of your employees to be your 2nd in command. Choose someone you trust, and can take your place in your absence. He or she can replace you while you are out on a business trip, vacation, sick at home, or when you are going to arrive late because of traffic, for example.

How do you choose that person?
How do you prepare and train for that person?

Choose the person in your team that has all the characteristics of being a leader. The one that others listen and go to when they need help. Be sure the person is reliable and does not break under pressure. I like my 2nd in command, to be honest, smart, to have initiative, talk straight, and open with me and know-how to improvise.

How do you trust someone to be your 2nd in command? He or She will have access to vital and sensitive information that, most of the time, cannot be shared. Trust is something that you earn. It takes time, commitment, and hard work.

If you have someone that has all those characteristics, then you need to involve him or her in the day-to-day business, including taking him or her to your meetings.

Start by assigning a small task that involves leading a small team in small low-risk projects and gradually empower him or her to start taking your place in more critical agendas.

One thing that is very important before you even start all the training. After you choose your "right arm" in your head, don't forget to ask him or her if they want to have that new role. Sometimes, even with the opportunity to move up on the career, some professionals do not want that responsibility and prefer to start doing what they do.

What about if you have two team members of your team that are precisely at the same level, which one do you choose for 2nd in command? Well, it depends. Probably one is more suitable than the other. If not, if they are both excellent candidates, you can do one of two things. One: you may have another 2nd in command and give both different tasks;
Two: have one as a reserve for when your 2nd in command is unavailable.

For you to be an effective leader, you need to have a second in command. Don´t try like I see many times do all on your own and never train anyone to be your "right arm" just because you don't have time or are afraid to lose your job. Yes, you heard me correctly, afraid to lose your job!

Some managers think if they train and empower an employee to be more familiarized with what they do, there is a chance they can become obsolete and lose their jobs. It is always a possibility if you are not a good manager or leader. A good manager knows its strengths and weaknesses.

A good manager will always try to improve on the weaknesses and perfect the strengths, and doing so avoids becoming obsolete. We are continually learning and the World, technology, trends are always changing. Don't be outdated. Keep up with the trends and be a trustworthy leader. One of the essential characteristics of a good leader is to know how to deal with people, how to talk, analyze, interact in a smart, healthy assertive way. This characteristic is one of the main differences between a leader and a boss.

One attribute I like in a 2nd In command and all my employees, in general, is for them to challenge me, to disagree with me, and show me their ideas and why they think I am wrong. I have seen too many times new processes fail because the person responsible for that new process never asked the experts, other employees, that do it for many years, what they think. They don't care about the input from other people. Sometimes they do even worst, they ask but don't give it any importance if it goes against their own believes.

Don't get me wrong. People will always be difficult and say things will not work when a new idea pops up. People are always resistant to change, but that does not mean you don't listen for what they have to say and work with them towards the new reality.

Chapter 2
ENGAGEMENT

INTRODUCTION

What is engagement? What does it mean for someone or a team to be engaged? Let's imagine. When someone says he or she is engaged and is going to marry, what does it mean engaged? If we think of a wedding, engagement is a free will desire to be with someone for the rest of your life. You are entirely focused, involved, and trilled to go ahead, marry, and commit yourself to be with the same person for the rest of your life. No one forced you to. When you are engaged, you go the extra mile for things to work out even in the roughest of times.

In the workplace, it is the same. You may have a team who does what you tell them to do, but if you don't explain all the steps and give them a clear deadline, they will just linger on.

An engaged worker or team will perform much better. They will go beyond what you asked them to do with minimum supervision and control. They arrive all motivated in the morning, ready to change the world. Usually, new employees are like that, and over time they will lose that motivation because they are not recognized, and things don't work out as expected. It is your job to keep your employees engaged in their work. How do you do that?

It is essential that the team members you lead feel inspired. They need to be engaged to perform better, go the extra mile and be happy doing their work. If they are not involved, their performance will start to decline. They will do the bare minimum and potentially leave the company.

So how do you engage your team members and keep them that way?

Many may think that a raise will solve the problem or a job promotion by itself. It is not only one factor, and most of the time, there is nothing to do with salary. So let's see one by one all factors that you need to have to keep your employees engaged.

That is what I will show you in this chapter.

GOOD WORK CONDITIONS

Figure 16 - Photo courtesy of bruce mars

Good work conditions can be many things, depending on if it is an office job, shop floor, or any other. If we think in an office job, to give good work conditions to your team, it is to provide them with, for example, the proper software/hardware to do their work efficiently. There is nothing more frustrating when you have a deadline, and your computer is always clashing and very slow. Don't let software or hardware get in the way of an employee's performing at his or her max.

Ergonomics is important. A suitable desk with enough storage space, proper room light, adequate room temperature, and a comfortable chair is essential. When working for many hours on a desk, if your employees don't have the proper posture and light, they will get tired very quickly and in pain. So after that, all the focus is not more on the work they are doing but how discomfort they are.

Let your employees personalize their place to make their space fill like home. Some like to bring plants, others collectibles or pictures. If it is nothing that goes against company policy is ok to let them personalize. If one day you have an important customer coming in, you can always warn the team to clean up their space as must as possible.

Have a functional break area with free coffee, refreshments, and small appliances for them to have a break.

Don't be too strict on cloth ethic. Let people be free to be themselves. I had a CEO that used jeans and a shirt. It was the way he was, and he was a great CEO. Of course, when he had to go to a business meeting or have distinguished guests, he would change the way he would dress. You can ask the same to your employees.

Many companies have the smart dress code from Monday to Thursday and go casual on Friday and that's ok. Some offices allow you to take your pets and that is ok as well. Try to make people feel like the office is their second home to a certain point.

Give them the right salary package, excellent benefits, flexible schedule, autonomy, job security, and proper workload. Don't let your employees go year after year with no salary increase and benefits.

THEIR WORK MATTERS

Figure 17 - Photo courtesy of Christina Morillo

Show your employees the impact of their work on the company. Show them their work matters, and because of all their commitment and sacrifice, the company was able to impress the customer and extend the contract, anything. Don't let your employees feel that they don't matter, what they do does not have any impact, and no one notices all their hard work and commitment.

Don't forget to mention your team or team members in meetings with management or emails showing they did an excellent job.

If you don't do this, they will feel obsolete, and eventually, their performance will start to decrease and ultimately leave or be laid off.

If you do meetings with your team every day to plan for the day and for them to give status on their current work, take the chance to thank them for their work and to continue a good job.

In chapter 3, I will discuss more in particular about the recognition of your team members and the entire team.

CLEAR CAREER PATH

Figure 18 - Photo courtesy of rawpixel.com

Most employees want to progress on their career or to change paths to try something new, and that is perfectly normal and something to be encouraged. But how do you define a career path for an employee?

First of all, you need to know your employees, his or her plans, and expectations.

I have monthly one to one meeting with my team members and I take that time to ask them what is their expectations in the future, where do they want to go? I have some that say they are ok as they are, others want to move up, and others want to do something completely different.

It is up to you to listen and explain you will do the best you can to try to open that door for him or her. Give a time frame to give some feedback about the request. Keep them updated, and if their claim is not possible, explain why and try to provide an alternative. They need to feel they are moving forward and not stuck in the same place all the time.

What if you have an employee that wants to be a lead or supervisor, and you know he or she doesn't have what it takes, for example? Let the employee know in this case, why he or she is not prepared to be supervisors or leads yet. Let them know how good they are and how experts they are in their field and even doubt they are not prepared to become supervisors, make them feel important by assigning them, and for example, to be the ones that mentor the newcomers. Make them responsible for small vital assignments. Pay them a trip to the manufacturing facility so they can see first hand what they have designed, for example. Many things can be done.

EMPOWER YOUR EMPLOYEES

Figure 19 - Photo courtesy of rawpixel.com

Empower your employees is like empowering your kids when they are growing up. You feed them all the knowledge, but you let them discover their way and do things the way they think is best.

Many managers micromanage their employees. There are also parents like that. Managers that micromanage their employees usually after giving them a task he or she will continuously supervise and make sure all the steps are done the way he or she should be done. Let me give you an example, you ask your kid to wash and clean the car, and you give him a time frame of 1-hour max.

The micromanaging parent will make sure he will start on the left, end on the right, vacuum first in the back, in a diagonal motion. Then wash the car, scrub like this like that, etc. This type of management leaves no much space for failure, but, at the same time, leaves no much space for learning and individuality. Do you know those kinds of parents that are on the sidelines of their kids' game always shouting, kick with the left, and the right, go back, move forward, etc. We all do.

There are micromanaging their kid during the game. A parent that does not micromanage will simply say what needs to be done in a certain amount of time and probably give some tips, but that's it. Then he leaves.
If your son or daughter did not do that well, or if we get back to the subject, your employee, be sure he or she will learn a lot from the mistakes and the advice you have to give after, and nothing replaces the sense of fulfillment they will have.

I also micromanage sometimes when necessary. If I have an urgent task that needs to be done in a short time and I have experience in it, I will ask one of my employees to do the job at hand, and I will give him or her specific instructions in every step of the way.

Micromanaging should be seen as a rare thing to use. Give the knowledge to your employees, let them grow and do things in their way. Supervise what they are doing, giving some tips, and help them whenever you can, but let them do the work in their way.

Encourage open discussions and disagreements. Let your team come to you and be comfortable saying they don't agree with you and why. When I say this, I don't mean having that employee that always disagrees with everything just because there is no reason for it, many times is only resistance to change. I give you an example. I had an employee that most of the time, did not agree 100% with me. He comes from a different business background and had open discussions with me stating his reasons and why he was not in agreement. We eventually get to an agreement. I do have these professionals in my team. He made me rethink things, see from a different perspective, and I loved it. This kind of employee that will challenge you will open your mind and give you new ideas that you will never get by yourself, alone.

Some employees will have more freedom than others. They will gain your trust and respect over time. I have some employees that I need to explain everything is small details. Leave the crumbs on the floor for him or her to follow till the finish. Others I just give them a task, a deadline, and that is it. They come to me with questions and ideas, and I am there to guide them and to listen.

Be a leader. Command your team to achieve a common goal.

HAVE ONE TO ONE TALKS

Figure 20 - Photo courtesy of Christina Morillo

One to one conversation with your employees are very important and useful. Avoid only having one once a year, and the best is to have one each month.

Many companies opt to have once a year evaluations, conversation with the employee and usually grade them for the entire year. It can work if you have a good record of how they did during the year, but you don't have their input during the year about their performance and how they feel about their career, the company all the changes coming in the future.

I have one to one meetings with my team members once a month, and I keep a record on our conversation. What should you discuss on these meetings? Why they are useful, how do they save money to the company and improve quality?

Let's see three scenarios.

First scenario: If you have an outstanding employee that is performing above what you expected;
Second scenario: If you have the average employee that is doing what you expect;
Third scenario: If you have an underperforming employee.

I divided into these three scenarios because the conversation you have on these three scenarios you're your employees is somehow different. The points to be discussed can be similar in some cases, but there will be specific differences. Remember, these conversations are from a perspective of engaging the employee to perform better and more motivated. In chapter 4, I will discuss when you have to move to disciplinary action when things do not improve.

Be sure you have taken the time to prepare yourself for the meeting. Get your quality matrix to see how the employee performed since the last month and take your notes from the previous session so you can follow up on any subject discussed before. If you don't give the proper preparation for this meeting, the employee will notice this is not that important to you and will just act as this is just a waste of time.

SCENARIO 1 – ABOVE AVERAGE EMPLOYEE

Ask your employee to sit and ask him how things are going on the day to day basis. Talk about currently undergoing projects. Ask what he or she thinks should be done differently, and if he or she experienced any challenges during the project.

Mention that you are pleased with his or her performance and that you know he or she is above average and is an essential member of the team.

Take this opportunity to give her or him more responsibilities and talk about career paths. Ask him or her if there are other assignments they are interested in and career aspirations.

By the end of the meeting, talk about areas of development, short and long term goals.

SCENARIO 2 – AVERAGE EMPLOYEE

The conversation will be similar to scenario 1 with some small tweaks.

Ask your employee to sit and ask him how things are going on the day to day basis. Talk about currently undergoing projects. Ask what he or she thinks should be done differently, and if he or she experienced any challenges during the project.

Mention that you are happy with his or her performance, but you would like him or her to improve here and there. Mention what he or she does best, his or her achievements and where he or she needs to improve. Be straight forward.

Take this opportunity to talk about career paths. Ask him or her if there are other assignments they are interested in and career aspirations.

By the end of the meeting, talk about areas of development, short and long term goals.

SCENARIO 3 – BELOW AVERAGE EMPLOYEE

The conversation is quite different depending on if the employee is performing below average most of the time or just recently.

3.1 – Constantly performing below average

Ask your employee to sit and ask him how things are going on the day to day basis. Talk about currently undergoing projects. Ask what he or she thinks should be done differently, and if he or she experienced any challenges during the project.

Mention that his or her performance is below expected for quite some time, and it has to improve.

Show him or her where they have to improve. Explain the consequences if there are no improvements in a small time frame. Usually, the next step is to put that employee under a PIP – Performance improvement program. (See about PIP on chapter 6)

Tell him or her in the end that you believe he or she can improve if they do the work and that you will support him or her as much as possible.

3.2 – Recently performing below average

Ask your employee to sit and ask him how things are going on the day to day basis. Talk about currently undergoing projects. Ask what he or she thinks should be done differently, and if he or she experienced any challenges during the project.

Mention that you notice his or her performance going down recently and ask him or her why that is.

Most of the time can be financial, health, or family issues that can lower the performance of an employee.

Have empathy for the employment situation, and ask if you can help in any way.

Remind the employee that you understand the situation, but you need her or his performance to go back up.

Give a time frame that you expect the employee to come back to have an acceptable performance.

BUSINESS TRIPS

Figure 21 - Photo courtesy of Pixabay

Depending on your business segment your employee's work, for example, the design of specific equipment on a computer, probably they never had the chance to see the real thing, the actual product.

Try to agree with your leadership business trips to the manufacturing site, for your employees to see the real product, to touch it, to be able to have the view of the factory employees and their feedback.

I have seen my team member's engagement growing exponentially together with their motivation and quality of work just by sponsor this kind of trip.

I am talking from an engineering point of view. If you think it is not viable to send people to those sites for any reason, try to bring the product to them. If that is not possible as well, what about having some video conferences with manufacturing where they can see the product live.

If possible, don't send one employee alone. It can be a little bit overwhelming, especially for younger employees. Usually, what we do in our company is every time a supervisor or manager has to travel to one of these sites, we book at least two engineers to go along and visit the site as well.

Plan their trip well. Give your team members assignments. Tell them what you expect them to do over there. Assign a mentor of that site to walk them around and show them the place.

Of course, you just send employees who are performing as expected or above expectations.

RECOGNITION WHO, WHEN, HOW

Figure 22 - Photo courtesy of bruce mars

You should recognize your employees every time they will do something extraordinary that helps a specific program, or colleagues, or even the entire company. It is imperative for your team members to fill engaged and that their efforts and initiatives are recognized.

Many managers have difficulties distinguishing when to recognize or not an employee and may even recognize an employee that was just doing the job he was hired.

It is essential to know who to recognize, the time frame to do that, and in what way.

- WHO -

Before you can decide who should be recognized, you have to define what is expected from every team member. It is important to remember what they were hired to do and their level of experience. If you are not sure or don't remember anymore, ask HR for their CV and the job advert.

You need as well to define how long usually a task or a step on your process takes so you can see without a doubt that an employee is performing above normal. For example, is a task usually takes two weeks and you have a member of your team that has done it in 7 days and maintain or increased the quality, that is something you should recognize.

Other than time-related recognitions also think about the quality of work. You need to define what is the expected quality and define what kind of quality increase you expect and consider normal for each employee. Above what you set is something that should be recognized. For example, you know from the past quality reports that it is expected to have an average of fifteen mistakes in a particular design. If an employee designs the same product in the same time frame for that task and has only seven errors, that is something to recognize.

So first, you need to line out what is expected so you can recognize a team member or call his or her attention for their lack of performance.

I have very well defined in a matrix all my team members. Their grades (a way HR determines seniority in the company I work), previous projects, their quality graded from 0 to 5, and how many days they needed to finish a specific design. All of my team members are different, in speed, in quality, so I have to evaluate them differently accordingly with their capacities, what they were hired to do, and their grades.

- WHEN -

The recognition should happen as soon as possible to the event in question. Don't wait until the end of the year. Do it while it's fresh. If you do it shortly after the event, the employees will try to go above and beyond their assignments during the entire year. If not, they will wait for the second quarter to even care.

With my team, I usually do it every three/four weeks. I have monthly one-to-one meetings with them individually about their performance and career path, and I take the opportunity to reward them on that meeting

There are some instances when I have an employee that had a breakthrough. For example, he or she invented a tool that helped the site and even the entire company for the better. If the employee agrees, the recognition is done in front of all other members of the team and site.

- HOW -

The how is very important and can have an impact on some team members on your team. You may have some team members that appreciate you recognize them in front of their colleagues or company, but you may also have others that don't like to be the center of attention and even run away from it. Know your employees and show them recognition in a way they will appreciate it.

I have an employee that was so stressed about being recognized publically that first, she stopped having initiatives, talking on meetings, and giving ideas. She was so uncomfortable with it that she started not showing to work when we had a town hall because she was afraid her name would pop up.

After I notice that, I asked management to stop announcing her name in the town halls. She is back performing above average, and every time I have to recognize her, I do it in my office, in a private conversation until she feels comfortable doing otherwise. This is an extreme and rare situation, but it may happen on your team.

You can recognize the entire team when a project ends, and as a team, the performance was above what was expected. You can take the team to lunch or have food catered in.

Chapter 3
MINORITIES

INTRODUCTION

In this chapter, I want to focus on minorities that you may have in your company, on your team, and how important it is to have diversity in the workplace.

I am working in the US in an office of 250 people, and only three, including me, are from outside the US, so you can say I belong to a minority. If you are the only woman in a group of 10 or more engineers, you are a minority. If you are Latino or African-American in a team where the majority is Caucasian, then you belong to a minority.

It is the job of the team leader and company to engage the minorities in the workplace, and there are several things you can do to achieve that and make everyone fill included, essential in your group, company, or even society.

So this is what I want to talk about this chapter.

DIVERSITY

Figure 23 - Photo courtesy of fauxels

Diversity empowers a company and its employees. Diversity will challenge current company standards, bring new perspectives to the meeting table, open-closed arguments, reinvent processes, break old habits, and revolutionary the way things are approached and though out. Many times makes the impossible into something tangible.

I have heard from several colleagues and professionals honest opinions about having diversity in their staff. Some more conservative think having diversity can have some advantages. It can also be a cause for incidents at work, arguments, discrimination, lack of trust, and that can damage business.

I don't agree at all with that perspective. The manager that shared that opinion with me was coming from a place where all workers are local. There were no outsiders, and a change in mentality can be challenging. Changing a company culture is not easy. It will cause a "riot" in the beginning, some people will leave, but the reality is, if a company does not have or allow to have diversity it will never survive in the market place, in the World as it is today.

Changes are never easy, and they always have resistance. You will need to be a strong leader to implement this kind of change in your company. Usually, you will see your employees go through four stages to change, denial, resistance, exploration, and finally, commitment. I will talk more in detail about these stages in chapter 4.

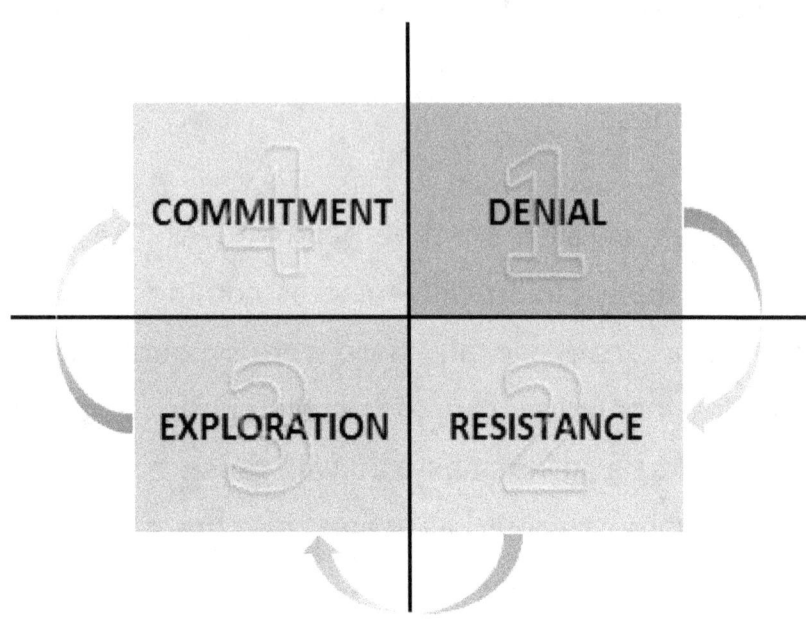

There are definite advantages to having diversity on your team and workplace as:

- More and better innovation;
- More variety of different perspectives;
- More creativity;
- Problems are solved faster;
- Decision making is more robust and superior;
- Employee engagement will increase;
- The employee turnover will reduce;
- Your department, the company will see an increase in profits and reputation.

Minorities usually feel left out, feel like Aliens on a different planet. I am an immigrant, and I know the feeling. It takes time, company and colleagues initiatives to start feeling included and one of the pack. Each one of us should take action to include minorities in the workplace. It can be in conversations or even meetings encouraging them to participate and sit at the table.

I have a team member that was a minority just for the fact she was the only woman in my team of 12 engineers. She rarely participated in the meetings and usually did not sit around the table. Often she would sit in a chair in the back of the room. So what can you do? I asked her to join the other around the table and encourage her to participate in the meeting. Enforcing her opinion was necessary.

Also, talk with your team, including the minorities, about trivial things, not only work and get to know them. It is like having a guest in your home, you want them to fill comfortable and like they are in their own home. Don't fall into the error of giving special treatment or advantages to minorities because the rest of your team will see that as privilege treatment.

One thing my company does when we have a foreigner worked staying with us for more than a few days. They will ask the company employees for volunteers to take them to lunch every day. That is a way to include people and make them feel welcome and not alone.

While we want diversity and encourage you to have it also, I do not support the idea some companies implement that you need a certain % of a minority group in your company as mandatory. Sometimes you have to do it because it is in your company policy, but I don't agree with it. I understand the company's perspective, they have an image that they need to show to the World, but what I know is that shareholders care about profit and results. If you don't hire the best of the best because of company policy, then you are in big trouble.

I think you should hire the best candidate you possibly can independently of the gender, age, race, color, or religion for a vacancy. That is my MO, and I have the luck to work in the company that thinks the same way, but at the same time, they encourage you to have as much diversity as possible.

EMPLOYEE RESOURCE GROUP

Figure 24 - Photo courtesy of fauxels

E very company has minority groups. You can even belong to one.

Usually, minorities get the support they need from their community, where they can find their peers, people who share the same beliefs, share the same language, have the same culture, religion, etc.

Many companies, usually big corporations, make available to employees an Employee Resource Group or ERG.

One of the ways you can include the minorities in your company is to suggest them to participate in this group.

Employee resource groups share a common diversity element or affinity, such as gender, sexual orientation, ethnicity, life stage (generation), or military service that are leveraged to build opportunities for networking, knowledge transfer, and professional development.

The ERGs started in the 60s as race-based forums that were created in response to the racial tensions on those times and since then evolved to include all types of professionals who want to join together in the workplace based on their characteristics or life experiences.

Affinity groups work to build an enhanced experience in the workforce, workplace, and marketplace through a unique lens fostering growth an innovation for the employee and enterprise.

Employee resource groups are designed to:

- Encourage personal and professional development
- Support and enhance the inclusivity of members and other employees into the organization

- Provide a constructive feedback forum for the broader Enterprise
- Engage in the recruitment and retention of underrepresented talent

If your company has ERG groups, I encourage you to join and participate. If there is no ECG group in your Country or State, tell HR you want to create one.

Usually, there are minimum requirements to do that, for example:

- You make your new ECG fall in one of the recommended categories pre-established.
- A minimum number of employees interested
- A certain number of members have to be at least for a specific time in the company
- Has to be sponsored by a higher manager

If your company does not have one, suggest creating the first one to your leaders.

SPONSORED EMPLOYEES

Figure 25 - Photo courtesy of Skitterphoto

Many companies sponsor employees with a VISA, so they can come and work for them. Usually, they are experts in their areas and have unique capabilities that cannot be found in the country the company is established.

They can come alone or with their family, and they usually need 2 to 3 years to adjust to the new country and society to start felling integrated. Some never fill integrated and is up to the companies to make them more involved in the community and the company.

These employees are considered a minority as well. If you belong to this group, talk with your company and enlist in an ERG group. If they don't have one group for Expats, immigrants, convince your company to create one.

I worked in several countries and worked for companies where I was considered a minority. I remember feeling alone, apart from all the others. As an example, I worked for three years in The Netherlands in the interior. Everything there was different, the language, culture, food, religion, humor, the notion of fun, etc. It took me quite some time to fit in.

The company I worked with did not have ECG groups. It did not help that the company was on the Country interior as well. So, before you accept a proposal to move to another country, make sure you will have social support from the community you are joining and at your workplace.

If you have Visa sponsored employees on your team, make them feel like one of the team. Take your team to lunch when you, all together, had a breakthrough or beat a deadline to celebrate and make sure everyone is having a good time as a team. It is up to you to make your team members feel included, empowered, important, necessary, unique, and at the same time, as one part of a successful team.

One thing a company I worked for did was to sponsor a soccer team made of company employees. Anyone could join, and I did as well, and that made all the difference for me. When you are doing sports as a team, everything changes. It is a perfect scenario to meet other people and to see what they are made off.

The company did a lot of other things to include families, employees, from food gatherings, games, and other things to get you out of your chair and interact with others in a non-work way.

People are people, so treat them as you would like to be treated.

Chapter 4
TEAM MANAGEMENT

INTRODUCTION

Lets talk about team management. When managing a team properly, there is no black and white solution. There are a lot of gray areas. All people are different, and you need to know each one of your team members very well. Use known technics but adjust them and let them be flexible for each team member.

In this chapter, I will talk about company policy, flexible time, promotions/career path, adapting to change, micromanagement, work tracking, and much more.

With this information, you will have more ammunition to fight everyday issues and to make your team feel secure because they have a reliable, consistent boss that has their back. At the same time, make your team members responsible for their shortcomings and their decisions.

COMPANY POLICY & PROCESSES

Figure 26 - Photo courtesy of Skitterphoto

All companies have policies that need to be followed. These policies mold the company culture. While we do our work, we have to follow processes that are designed to maintain quality, and things go smoothly and done correctly at the first time. The question is, can we bend a little the company policies or get a little out of the process if we know it will improve quality or team morale?

Seems simple the response, right? Should be a straight no. Company policies and processes are to be always followed. But are there exceptions? Maybe, it depends on how you look at things and how much flexibility you management gives you and the subject in question and its urgency. If policies and processes are well written, they will have a solution for exceptional cases in certain circumstances.

The key is if you need to bend the rules a little, you have to contact all the key players that are responsible for these processes or company policies to know if they agree with you.

- COMPANY PROCESSES -

I am an Engineer manager, and I always follow the processes defined and approved by governance. It happens often, and especially if you have a house that sets these rules to other sites to follow, processes do not work 100% as intended. Maybe they work for the corporate site and improve speed and quality, but perhaps it will not to another site. It is easy to go around processes and make things move fast and with quality because you know better, you know the product, you know the customer and you have the experience and you did not get a say when this process was written.

Besides, it is also tempting to go around the current process if you are pressured with schedule, and you know you can have the product complete is a couple of days instead of a couple of weeks. For me, worse than going around a non-working process when you are against schedule is following a mandatory process, and there is no quick way to fix it, or it is impossible to have the authorization to do it differently. Basically, there is nothing you can do.

The biggest mistake I see on companies and their processes is not having a fast and quick way to fix the existing defective process. You don't need to go and revise a 300-page process every time you have to update it a little and then wait for ten people to agree with it and sign it. You can have a simple process where a memo is written, a deviation document mentioning the changes in the current process, and have only a few people signing it. After several memos or deviations from the process, you can revise the document and add all the updates.

It seems simple right? , but many companies don't do it, and it is incredible how professionals responsible for writing and approving these processes trough money out

out the window. Usually, they don't move faster because they are not aware of its impact or don't want to show they were wrong in the first place, or maybe they don't have time because they are involved in 1000 different things. Everything is money in a company, especially time. Think about it, did you work for a company that had more meetings than time to do the work? Sometimes they are necessary, but most of the time, they are not required or not well planned to make them productive and short.

When you book a meeting, you should be aware of its cost. For example, on average, if everyone in the meeting costs to the company $100 /hour, if you do a meeting with ten people for 2 hours to get nowhere, you just spent your company $2000, doesn't seem much but if you have meetings all the time. On an international level, you do the math.

You should be able also to calculate the dollars spent while a design gets on hold because the process does not work, or there is only one person that can do anything about it, and it is traveling or on holidays.

In summary, processes should always be followed, and you should not deviate from that unless you have direct instructions from a person above your food chain that can back you on that. It is imperative to have a defined process to update existing ones, a quick, fast track way to do that.

I give you an example. I worked in a company where we had a change process to change a design that had an issue in production. It could take 2-3 weeks to make that change, from the finding to the actual closing. Today, I work in a company that can do that in 8 hours, 8 hours! It is the same exercise. What changed was the process. It is much smoother, and it was written involving all the key members and finalized by experienced managers.

We need to have more ethical, courageous, managers with integrity, directors that are not afraid to change the company core and fight for what they think is right and especially make people accountable for their mistakes.

- COMPANY POLICY -

I am not a rebel or a rode manager that does not follow the rules. No, that is not me, and that is not what I want you to do. Like every policy, they are elaborated to work most of the time, to make everyone roar to the same side.

Although company policies should not be broken, I believe that in particular cases it is ok to bend them a bit to reward your best employees. Let me give you an example.

One of my company policies mentioned that every employee needs to do 40 hours a week, Monday to Friday. We had a flexible schedule and an honored time in and out system. Sometimes I would let a good employee work only 34-36 hours in the week and let him do the extra hours next week. Another example is if he or she worked extra or longer hours, I would give him or her half a day off. You can do a lot of things, and that will go a long way with your employees.

There is the other side of the coin, and you need to be aware of it and firm with your team. Some employees will take advantage when you make these exceptions. Some employees think because one has an exception, he or she should have it also and will ask for it even when they do not deserve it. Explain why it was given to the other employee and how he or she can also have the same benefits if he or she also has the same performance. Be very clear that he or she can also get it because there are no special employees. They are just awarded by their quality of work and goals met.

There are also other types of employees, the ones that, for example, book things in advance and then let you know that they need to miss a specific day, and since they made extra hours, they are entitled to it. I have no problem giving a day off to an employee that made extra hours, but it depends on why he or she made those extra hours. If an employee made extra hours and worked from Monday to Thursday the 40 hours and want Friday off and those extra hours were to put off a fire, an emergency, a delivery we have to do to a customer urgently, of course, he or she will have the day. If an employee made extra hours in a week and wants a half-day off, but those extra hours were necessary for him or her to deliver their work on time, and they were late because they let things till the last moment, then no, no time off is granted. You just need to open the rules of the game for all and say no when needed.

I am going back to the employees that book things in advance. I had an employee that book a flight and hotel to visit his brother and just come to my office to let me know, and since he made extra hours on the weekend should be no problem. Wrong. You, as a manager, decide if you give days off or not, not the other way around. I let him go on the trip, and I warn him that this was not ok and that he has to let me know in advance that he wanted to come work on the weekend to compensate for an extra day on the week after.

These are just some examples. Be sure to discuss this bending of rules with your manager to have his or her authorization.

FLEXIBLE TIME

Figure 27 - Photo courtesy of Stas Knop

Some companies offer their employees flexible time. If they need to do 40 hours a week, for example, they can choose the schedule to fulfill that with certain limits that usually are referenced in the company policy. You don´t have to do 8 to 5 everyday day. You can enter early, get out sooner, take a couple of hours out to go to the bank, and many other ways. Of course, you still need to deliver your work on time, with quality and attend meetings.

Studies found that employees are looking for benefits first, above salary, especially flexible work, even leaving jobs because their work is not flexible.

There are pros and cons on the employee side as well on the employer side, in my opinion. There is a lot of information online, but this is what I observed:

	EMPLOYERS	EMPLOYEES
PROS ✓	<ul><li>Less turnover</li><li>Less absence</li><li>Boost morale</li><li>Increases engagement</li></ul>	<ul><li>More time with family</li><li>Less commute time</li><li>Feel more in control</li><li>Increases engagement</li></ul>
CONS ✗	<ul><li>Less supervision</li><li>A feeling of lack of control</li><li>Lack of coverage*</li></ul>	<ul><li>No clear division between work and home time</li></ul>

*Lack of coverage – there may be times during the day there is no one available for a task.

Some companies go even the extra mile, you have flexible time, you have to do 40 hours a week, and you don't have to sign in or out of the office. The time is not controlled by anyone other than you. It is called the honor system. As well there are pros and cons on when using the honor system above the flexible one:

	EMPLOYERS	EMPLOYEES
PROS ✓	• Cost-effective* • No need to control in and out	• Feel empowered • Feel trusted and engaged • Feel less control, treated like honor adults
CONS ✗	• Cheating employees • No checking system for several hours, especially extra time • Difficult to prove to cheat	• The unfair feeling when an employee cheats the system • No way to prove in and out time if questioned

*Cost-effective – it was determined that the cost of enforcing proper counting of work hours is higher than using the honor system even when you have employees cheating the system.

Then we have entirely flexible companies. You can choose where to work, when to work and decide how many hours and days you work as well. You work solely defined with objectives, specific date to end a particular project, and it is entirely up to you how to get there. In this case, I believe it only works in specific projects or businesses. You just have to be sure you go and work to a company that fits your needs. There will always be advantages and disadvantages, but in the overall, flexible time is one of the big "look for" by the job seekers.

Many organizations in Europe are implementing the four working days per week, and many countries in Europe by law work between 30-35 hours a week, depending on the country. They are still debating the advantages and disadvantages of those policies. Nevertheless, company owners who adopt this kind of measure say they were able to increase production, quality, and above that, the morale of the employees increased. How can that be? One less day or fewer hours a week and more productivity? I believe that some ideas only work in certain countries and cultures. It is directly connected to the way we are, what makes us tick, and our moral compass.

Let me give you an example. I worked in an Automotive company in Europe and had branches in Brazil and Africa. I received my paycheck every month, but the subsidiaries in Brazil paid the workers weekly. In Africa, there was a factory they were paid daily. The reason for this is that they knew if they paid the employees monthly or weekly, the employees would not show up to work for days or weeks. This is a clear example of cultural differences.

Even when it is for the best, change of processes, habits, to make them a success takes time, commitment, perseverance, and understanding.

CHANGE

Figure 28 - Photo courtesy of fauxels

Change. People usually don't like change. They want what is comfortable, what is working for them now, what they know and feel they can predict. Most people will retaliate when there is a change in the company policy or processes, for example. Change is unavoidable and necessary for a company to grow, to update itself to the changing world, to be ahead of change. Employees usually fear change because they think it can affect their job security, can add extra work to their plate, and make them obsolete. It is your job as a team manager to prepare your team and to guide them through the change with optimism and the truth.

Always expect resistance to change and negativity. There are some predefined stages an employee will go through until he or she is fully engaged with the new idea, new process, and change in general. These stages are not autonomous, and you cannot sit and wait for the employee to go from one stage to the other by him/herself. It is your job to help him to go from one stage to another. Let me show you how.

Let's look at one of the existing change acceptance models:

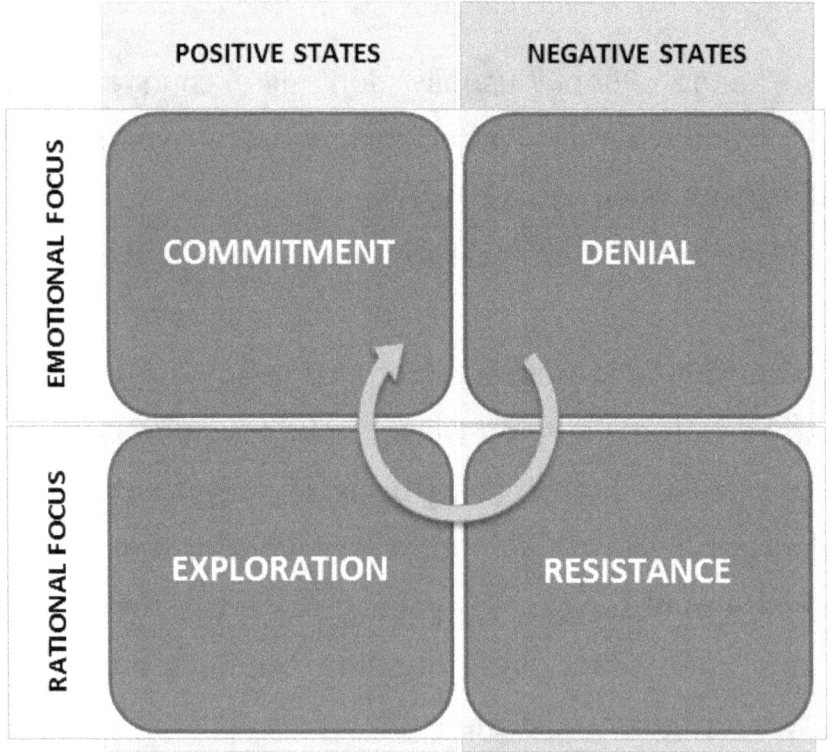

When a change is presented to the employee, he or she will pass through 4 stages in this order:

Denial, Resistance, Exploration and Commitment.

This model does not fit all employees but fits the majority. There are, of course, employees that will go directly to exploration and commitment, but they are a tiny percentage.

So let's check one stage at a time and see what can be done to help move to the next stage and what are the signs that an employee is on a particular stage.

These stages have similarities with the five stages of grief by Elizabeth Kubler-Ross:

STAGE 1 - DENIAL
STAGE 2 - ANGER
STAGE 3 - BARGAINING
STAGE 4 - DEPRESSION
STAGE 5 - ACCEPTANCE

So we can say an employee when dealing with a substantial change may experience some kind of grief.

But let's look now at each stage of the change acceptance model.

PHASE 1 - DENIAL

Denial or Shock is the first stage of change. The information of a change is received trough rumors, grapevines, or official channels. The denial or shock is a very natural reaction to change and usually what you ear is:

- "This will not work, was tried before";
- "Why is this happening?";
- "This will go away, I am sure it will blow over soon";
- "This change does not affect me".

Usually, people going trough change will avoid the topic, especially if they are male. Females tend to exteriorize more, talk more about the subject. They will slow down and only do routine work and blame others for the difficulties they are experiencing.

Managers and team leaders during this phase should have as much face to face conversations as possible and explain what they will have to gain with this change. Their objective is to have people out of Denial as soon as possible. Things will slow down. People need time to embrace change. You need to give them space and time for that. So my advice is, accept the change, plan that things will take 1/4 time longer to do because people need time, and this phase is inevitable.

Remind people on your team that the door to your office is wide open, and they can come and talk to you as much as they need. Keep them in the loop and informed on any updates.

PHASE 2 - RESISTANCE OR/AND ANGER

After sensing this change does not go away, the employees will go from denial to resistance. Usually, they can't see a way out situation, so they turn to anger most of the time. This change now becomes personal. No more "this change does not affect me".

Discuss with your team why they feel resistant to this change. They experience loss. Your team feels they lost power, control, security, comfort, value, expertise, or any other kind of loss. Usually, they have concerns about new changes, responsibilities, and if they will be up to the challenge.

Some people take longer than others to pass this phase, and that is perfectly normal, but be aware of those who seem to stay stuck on this phase, they will demonstrate passive-aggressive behavior.

You can usually see this kind of behavior as well:

- doubt themselves and their decisions;
- complain more than usual;
- can become very quiet and unresponsive;
- say "this will never work" or "they should involve all in this kind of decisions, they don't know what they are doing";
- loose initiative;
- talking about the past and all the issues they faced.

As a manager and team leader, make sure to have at least one open channel, but more would be advised and talk with your team regularly, focusing on their concerns. Similar to the denial phase, you need to give people time to accept the change. Help your team focus in the future, the road ahead, embrace the past, but do not focus on it, and remember we are all in the same boat and need to roam in the same direction.

PHASE 3 - EXPLORATION

Employees will step in this phase when they accept that the change is necessary. Sooner or later, it will become clear these changes are required. At this point, employees will try to compromise an outcome that is favorable to them. They are more than half-way of the change process. They don't think anymore that the change is not possible and/ or will make things worse, but in what can I do to help the transition.

Employees are ready to go, to learn new skills if necessary, and seek new ideas. Many times they get overwhelmed with everything new they need to know or adjust and may experience some stress and anxiety at this point.

Try to communicate timelines, ask everyone to get involved, have a brainstorm, and be completely clear and visible in what is needed to be done.

In this phase, employees are full of energy. They want to learn and solve problems. Still, they need guidance, otherwise, that energy will dissipate into space, and people can get frustrated and depressed if you don't help them keep the motion, grab their ideas, involve them in the entire process and let them know that this change will only work with their help, commitment, and input. Encourage people that are in this phase to help colleagues that are still stuck in the resistance phase.

In this phase, managers need to be facilitators, guide employees, and their energy, helping them work together to come out of this change stronger and more powerful. Change can be a boost to your team as it can be a demoralizing event. It is up to you to set the mood.

PHASE 4 – COMMITMENT

Congratulations. Your employees did the entire cycle and are now at the commitment phase. They chose to accept the change and now can work efficiently again. If you did things correctly, your employees are motivated, relieved, feel more energetic, and have a stronger sense of belonging.

The first change is always the hardest and most important one. If the first change went ok, they are now empowered to go much faster through a second change.

Take advantage of this stage to repeat and reinforce the new objectives and strategies. Go through the lessons learned while going through the change. Don't forget to celebrate the success and reward people on this phase

STRATEGIC THINKING

Figure 29 - Photo courtesy of fauxels

Strategic thinking, as the name says, has to do with thinking while using strategies to be the full picture and make the right decisions. This is an ability that you can learn with time and apply it to everything, business, or personal life. When your strategic thinking you look at things is a small and big scale as in the long and short term. You also have to think about the past, the present, and try to "guess" what the outcome you want in the future will be.

This skill is increasingly important when you climb up the ladder on the organization and essential if you have career aspirations.

Remember when you start working? To get that promotion, the only thing you needed was to do an excellent job in your given task, on time and quality, without questioning it. It was like that in school as well to get good grades. In school, you were not expected to challenge the professor but to learn from him and do as he instructs you to do.

You can progress at some point like this, but at a certain point in your career, you will notice you will not evolve anymore, you are stuck. You need to come out of the box, to talk, to challenge your boss for new ideas, challenge your colleagues and go beyond and have an open mind what you can come up with that will help you, department and business.

"What got you here won't get you there" by Marchall Goldsmith.

You are going to need to change the way you think and start thinking strategically. It will not be a one-time thing that you do. It is a change in behavior, planning, and strategy. See this, like learning a new skill or language. It requires work, dedication, and time.

To start thinking strategically, to open the Pandora box to your brain, start questioning things, practices, and habits and why things are done in a certain way and not in another way. Do this alone, or in a group, new ideas will emerge. Some of them will not be useful, but in the end, you will have new ideas that will help you, your department or business. Think about how the airplanes were when first invented and how they are now. Did someone ask why wood? Why two pairs of wings? Can we make it lighter? Go higher and faster?

From the business perspective, you probably have a process you follow to design or manufacture a product, and it works, but why not look the all process from start to beginning and ask why we do things this way and try to improve the process.

You need to stop working and be busy all the time. Yes, you heard me, right! You need to stop and observe what goes around you, place the entire process on a whiteboard, and see the big picture.

Then you need time, quiet to reflect and come with new ideas. I know what you think that you don't have time for that, you are very busy doing a million other things. You need space or time where no one interrupts you, and you can think about what you learned and observed. Book a time later Friday evening when everyone already left. One hour a week is already a good starting point.

Don't see strategic thinking only at a business scale or meant only for executives and senior managers. Still, it is also for you as an individual as a leader and something to teach and encourage your team members. Everyone should take time and space for strategic thinking.

If you want you and your team to start thinking strategically, you have to think more than the present. Learn with the past and evaluate the trends and different scenarios in the future.
Ask yourself the whys and the whats regarding the past to learn from possible mistakes or breakthroughs. If something went wrong in the past, investigate what happened, do a route cause analysis until you have all the answers.

For the future just right down, map, what are all the possibilities for the future. It is not possible to see in the future, but with experience, you will be more able to pinpoint more precisely what will be the outcome. Analise as well the macro trends, for example, space tourism, and see how that can affect your business.

If you know influential people, journalists, professors, talk with them regularly to have an idea what the future reserves. Good strategic thinkers also read a lot, are well informed about what happens in the world.

WAR BOARD

Figure 30 - Photo courtesy of fauxels

One of my daily routines with my team is a stand-up meeting that usually lasts 5 min. I have one meeting in the morning and one at the end of the day if necessary. The objective of this daily meeting is to keep a rhythm, to keep the team focus on the current project, and get current updates on the work at hand. This standup is an opportunity for you to address any issue that needs to be escalated or find a solution to a problem to meet schedule.

These meetings usually take place next to a board, a War Board, where every step, phases, steps, dates, actions, action owners are displayed and are updated daily.

You can use a whiteboard to write on it, a magnetic whiteboard to use magnets, post-its, whatever works for you. The important thing you need to remember is that the board is not only for you but for everyone passing by. Your managers should be able to look at it in your absence and see exactly where everything is and when it will be completed, all the issues and solutions.

I especially like to use a whiteboard with magnets. You can quickly move the pieces and change the board from one project to another.

In my company, there are several WAR BOARDS. As an example, a project where the objective was to design a new vehicle has an electrical team, mechanical team, structures, and many others. In the center is the program manager board. The program manager board sets the pace, the overall schedule, and all gates to be met. For example, it has dates for PDR – Preliminary Design Review and CDR – Critical design review. The other board, as per instance, the mechanical one, will have all the stages of the mechanical design necessary to achieve to reach the first gate PDR.

When on the board make sure you encourage people to give you a proper update and not just say all is going as planned and the day before the deadline you find out that the schedule is going to be missed because of an issue that if solved right on the beginning would not be an issue.

Make people accountable for not giving you a truthfully, detailed update and recognize those who do. Ask the proper questions to help those who are not good at providing all the details or just shy. You need to know everything that is going on on those 5 mins and what is the way forward.

Encourage your team to update the board themselves every time there is an update, and you can discuss it on the next stand-up.

Empower people during these meetings, acknowledging, for example, a gate that was achieved sooner than expected but never reprimand your team members in front of the colleagues. Call him a few minutes later to your office and talk with him or her. There is no need to humiliate anyone, and it will work against you and will lower the performance of that employee.

One thing that helps speed these meetings up in large groups, especially in shop-floor environments, is to have a sticker with their name in the floor so when they show up to the meeting they are always in the same place, and you are not looking in the crowd where that person is.

The consequences of not having a follow up with a daily stand-up meeting can be catastrophic. When you think all is going well, you find out in the end that there is a lot of issues that need to be tackled and not enough time. Other consequences for not having the daily standup are a decrease in the product design quality, and the time to make things done increases significantly.

Don't mistake the WAR BOARD with the WAR ROOM. WAR BOARD is a stand-up meeting that takes between 5-10 minutes. A WAR ROOM is where a design team meets, to have a brainstorming event, to have open discussions, and find new ways to do things better. This type of activity can last hours or days.

If you don't have standups in your company or war board, try it on your next project, it will be worth it.

MERITS

Figure 31 - Photo courtesy of Gustavo Fring

Most companies go through the merit season where you decide if your employees deserve a salary increase or not. Usually, you don't give a salary increase to people that are under a PIP – Personal improvement program or that generally underperform.

The merit season is once a year, so don't make the common mistake in deciding for an increase or not just by looking into the previous couple of months. You have to evaluate that employee entire year. There are several ways you can keep a record of their performance. For instance, you have or should have regular, monthly one-to-one conversations, and you should make a record of their performance. You also have the yearly goals they have to achieve. Another way to keep records is to evaluate them for every project they do.

I give you my example. This year my team did not perform so well on the last project that lasted two months. The process was imperfect, but they made mistakes they shouldn't do at this point. I gave them a merit increase. I spent all my budget on giving them a good rise that ranged from 3-4%. I did that because I know them, I follow their work, and know-how dedicated they are. I have their entire year evaluation. If I didn't, I would probably be reluctant to give them the increase. So you must keep a record, some metrics on how your team members are doing.

So, how do you decide how much should the increase be? How do I know if I should give 3% to one and 4% to another?

Well, this was my line of thought for this year.

1 – Gave 0% to one employee that is under a PIP because his performance is deficient and did not improve.

2 - I grabbed 3/4 off all my budget for merit and divided equally by the rest of the team.

3 – Checked all the annual salaries and gave more merit to my best performers, especially those that have a lower salary compared with others that do not perform as well.

4 – Gave the standard 3% to one of my team members just because he relies a lot on the help of others but still performs well.

BUILD BRIDGES

Figure 32 - Photo courtesy of Klaus Tauberman

Allies. You need allies, mentors, partners, people who are happy with your success, who want to help you move further and can give you a hand in case of need. This World is challenging to navigate. We tend to do things by ourselves and don't trust anyone else. You can succeed by yourself, but it is much harder and takes much more time for you to get where you imagine yourself to be in the future.

Nowadays, it is complicated to trust entirely in someone else other than friends and family members. In the workplace, when you start going up the ladder, you begin to be a target, and many people want you to fail and fall on your face. It is very easy to get to a point where you don't trust anyone anymore, but you should try in small dosages to test people, and gain some confidence back.

I have seen many people going into a path where they isolate themselves and above that burn bridges with other people. What do I mean to burn bridges? If you get mad and trough someone over the bus, that person will not trust you anymore. The "bridge" has burned between you and that person, and the free will cooperation is gone. You never know when you are going to need that contact, that person in the future. Be respectful always, avoid pointing your fingers in front of other people, to enter in the spin of the blame game. Don't fly as well on another person's wing. You should fly on your achievements and not from others.

I believe in Karma, and I have seen it too many times, sometimes instantaneous, other times it takes years, but life will always catch you to bring you the bill for the wrongdoings you did.

I believe I am a good leader for my team, I respect them all, encourage them all to go further and a few to take my place one day, but I can't say I had a manager that did the same for me. I had managers that used my talent to help themselves look good while I was just getting some minor attention, appreciation, or promotion.

I always had more luck and better relationships with bigger fish. For some reason, I was good at building bridges with CEOs, Directors, and other top managers because I was never afraid to speak with them directly if I had an idea or concern. Many years forward, many of them still recall me and the good work I did in a particular project.

SURVEYS

Figure 33 - Photo courtesy of fauxels

How do you know if you are doing an excellent job as a manager? How do you know where your misses are and where you need to step up. You can for sure see if your management and people skills are doing the work by watching how your team is performing and on your one to one´s meeting, but there are always things that will be difficult for you to see, and you have two ways to know that. As someone said one day, it is easy to evaluate yourself when you see yourself from the outside.

One way for you to know your shortcomings is when your manager keeps you up to date on how you are performing in your position. If you have an honest manager that likes to help you, this is the best place to get feedback on how you are doing. Indeed it is a good source, but the only way to get the truth is from your team in how you are doing and how do they perceive you as their manager. If you informed them correctly of the company changes, how you lead through rough times, if you have in mind their careers, if you listen, empower them in a summary if you make them feel they can count on you and are part of the company.

The way to know all this is by doing anonymous surveys. I have some team members that defy me and tell me things as they feel in private, and I really appreciate those employees, but then you have those that are scared to tell you what they think because they think they will be put aside or worst.

I thought I was doing a great job as a manager. My team seemed happy, working well, meeting deadlines, I was empowering them, giving them more responsibilities, promoting, awarding, and reprimanding with tact, but I was wrong. The best thing that happens to me was my company decided to start these anonymous surveys. I found out a lot about myself and my management skills and strategy.

Some of the things I learned from my team feedback were that I was always busy to listen genuinely and that I didn't follow up on their ideas. It was eye-opening. I started to listen more, stop what I was doing, not interrupting, and just listening and listening more. On the other hand, because I was always too busy, I was not giving the proper attention to some of their ideas, not seeing them as urgent or following upon them. You should fight for your team ideas if they are right, whatever obstacles you find in the way.

I am glad I was able to know these things and change my ways. In the next survey, I was able to score higher, and those kinds of comments disappeared.

My only regret was not starting the survey idea sooner, without waiting for the company to impose it. You can begin with your own department survey. You just need a box and ask them to fill a questionnaire, and you are on your way to becoming a better manager.

Chapter 6
DISCIPLINARY ACTIONS

INTRODUCTION

Disciplinary actions are one of the responsibilities of any leader/manager. For me, it is one that is essential to apply when it is really necessary. I like to avoid doing it, and I can even say I dislike doing it. I see many managers look the other way and don't apply any disciplinary action at all. When disciplinary action is used well, it will prevent your team from starting underperforming, and it will send a message to your team that you are not there only to award or to manage projects at hand but to discipline as well.

PERFORMANCE IMPROVEMENT PLAN (PIP)

Figure 34 - Photo courtesy of Christina Morillo

Performance improvement plan or PIP is a process that you need to master if you want to put a team member that is lacking on his or her work, back on track. That should be the primary purpose of this plan. This plan will also register that you and the company made every attempt to keep the employee before you have to decide to let him or her go. It works as proof in the case that employee sues the company for being laid off unlawfully.

As per definition, the Performance Improvement Plan (PIP) is a process used to fix persistent performance problems supported by the documented procedures. This process should be used with the support of human resources and includes current and expected performance, timelines, measures of performance improvement, and potential outcomes based on whether or not sufficient improvement is achieved. This process should allow an employee who is not meeting expectations the opportunity to succeed or the manager to prepare for progressive disciplinary actions.

As said, this process is not a guarantee that your team member will improve, but it is a way to deal with the issue. The person in question has two options, to improve or be laid off. Not very often, but it happens sometimes, you just have the wrong person in the wrong place. The employee can be doing poorly on one position and excel on another, so be open to the possibility of moving a person internally before letting him or her go.

It is your job to ensure your team delivers a product or service with quality on time. It is also your job to train, guide, and empower your team, so they are enabled to deliver what you expect from them. It is as well your responsibility to let someone go that is not delivering what they were hired to do.

I am going to show you how you should do a proper PIP and show you two real story examples I had in my department.

Where to start? First, you need to know who needs a PIP, and how do you do that? It has to be someone that is not performing as expected for what they were hired for, for example. You need to have a record of their performance over time for 2-6 months, depending on your company, and it has to be really measurable, specific, not just a table saying he has done well this month and not so well on the other. For example, if your employees design a product that is reviewed by experts, count the number of findings, problems, and see if they continually repeat the same mistakes or if the number of findings goes up.

One thing I probably should have mentioned before is if you have a good employee that all of a sudden starts to decline, have a talk to him or her to see what is going on and if you can help before beginning the PIP.

Now let us get into it. First, you need to write or have HR give you a letter that you will provide to the employee. This letter explains the process, for how long it will happen, the outline expectations, and usually mentions that excelling on the PIP is not a guarantee of employment. It needs to say as well that if they don't meet expectations, termination of employment may occur. It seems cold, but it is necessary to avoid lawsuits.

Now it is time to follow the performance improvement plan:

DIAGNOSE

- Measure and evaluate employee performance (results & behaviors)
- Documentation (notes, emails, memos, anything) of ongoing performance feedback (formal & informal)
- Make sure the employee knows that his or her current performance is not acceptable, requires improvement and you are there to help
- Review performance data with HR

COMMUNICATE

- Give continuous and timely feedback to make sure the employee understands expectations (goals, objectives, KPI, measures, stepbacks). Have a one to one at least once a week to communicate how she or he is performing.
- Let the employee knows that his or her current performance is not acceptable, needs to be improved, that you know he or she will succeed and that you are there to help. Explain as well what can be the implications if the performance does not improve

PREPARE THE PLAN

- Prepare documentation that will guide the process and show the progress.
- Have a specific column on that document to show what improvements are required, what is the action needed for those improvements to start showing, the

target date for each activity, the duration of the PIP, how often you should have progress reviews and don't forget to have everything signed by you and the employee in question.
- At this stage also p
- `lane the letter you are going to send to the employee with HR
- Include the effective date and PIP duration
- Include frequency of reviews
- Include a plan of action
- Don't forget to include as well the consequences

COMMUNICATE THE PLAN

- Optionally with the HR present or your superior manager, you will present the letter and plan to the employee. The HR or manager present is to prevent an awkward or unpleasant situation if the employee gets in a heated argument.
- Preferably partner with HR on how to communicate with the employee and to prepare the message to be delivered.

MONITOR THE PLAN

- You will schedule a weekly meeting to evaluate the progress with the employee (optionally you may have HR present)
- Documentation of each progress review:

- What specific improvement/development needs have been identified?
- What improvement/development actions are to be taken? What other support is required?
- How is success measured?
- Date each action will be complete

CONCLUDE THE PLAN

At this point, you have three possible outcomes:
- Successful completion and remain in the current position.
- Unsuccessful Completion:
  - Involuntary Termination Process
  - Demotion
  - Move to a different department

Usually, the outcome for the unsuccessful completion is job termination. Still, it happens, rarely, that an employee will be happy to move to another department that he or she fits best or to be demoted since he or she was more satisfied with the previous position. I had an employee that was one of my best, was promoted to a leading position where she failed utterly. He was also more stressed, unhappy, more uptight, so when she ended the PIP with no success, I gave him the option to return to his previous position where she was pretty good at. He was more than happy to do it. It is rare because most people will be unhappy, mad, and will damage the company by contaminating the team and work If they stay.

Don't take your decision lightly, think, know your employees, don't reflect only on the current performance of that employee but the entire history so you can decide the case of the unsuccessful completion of a PIP.

Be aware that in some cases of successful completion of the PIP, employees will return to the behaviors that have put them in the PIP in the first place. If this happens, let HR know what is going on, and usually, the way is to move that person to the status of unsuccessful completion. Bad habits are not easy to change, it is reasonable they go back to some bad habits, and you need to let them know right away it is not ok and wait some time for the change to come but if the bad habits are systematic and nothing changes you need to contact HR.

LAYOFFS

Figure 35 - Photo courtesy of Anna Shvets

L ayoff is the word no one wants to ear. It is a dreadful moment when you know the company will have to layoff employees, and that includes members of your team. I have worked for companies that, in my opinion, dealt very well with layoffs and others that were horrific and without any concern about the employees. In this topic, I am going to show the options companies can opt before laying off employees, but my main concern is to let you know how you should prepare and how you should tell the news to your employee. In many cases, the HR representative will give the news, but you will be present, preferably.

Before I start to go deeper into how you should manage the layoff process, here are some initiatives US companies can opt for. I say US companies because the EU has different labor laws and maybe these options do not apply:

Relocation

See if there is any other opening on the company or in any other site in the US where the employee will fit and offer that option to him or her before you opt to layoff. I have seen some companies layoff, experienced employees, without even considering the option, and it is a reliable option that can easily be a win to win situation.

Hire freeze

No more hiring. One of the earlier solutions a good company would follow is to freeze all hiring. There are always some specific cases that they can open an exception if they have an essential contract, and they need someone with particular skills that can't be found inside the company.

No merit or salary increase that year

To froze the merit or salary increase. This is another solution that the company can follow to slow down the losses. You need to explain to your team that these measures are required to try not to layoff employees.

Salary reduction

This hurts your team members' feelings. I have seen cuts of 10% in some companies on the salary, and usually, they will give some paid holidays in return. A 10% cut on the wage is better than no job. Still, many people live month to month on their budget, and 10% can make a huge difference. Have empathy and talk to your team members explaining the situation the company is going through and the losses they are having.

Layoff contractors

One measure I saw companies do is to layoff all contractors after giving them the option to be permanent. If you are a contractor, you know the risk of your job to be cut short when things get ruff, or a particular project ends. The primary objective of the company is to prevent layoffs on the permanent staff.

Voluntary leave

Voluntary leave announcement is a prediction that layoffs are a good possibility. The company has a number in their mind of the number of people they need to layoff. First, they try to see if anyone above 55 years old and more than ten years in a company will leave voluntarily with the right package. This option works for those who are thinking of getting earlier retirement to pursue something else, something on their own. You can try to find another job or even ask for unemployment benefits in most cases.

Furlough

Leave without pay. You have a job, and benefits like medical but no pay. Workers are eligible for unemployment benefits during this time. This decision usually is not taken lightly by any company that respects its employees.

The layoff of permanent employees

I am going to try to guide you on how you should handle this situation.

Unless you are very high in the chain, usually the news of layoff will come a few days before it happens or generally in the day before it happens. When this happens, I am briefed that a member of my team was chosen to be layoff and why. I am asked to keep it a secret and told when the dismissal is going to happen.

Let me tell you to step by step how it rolled down to me a few years ago. I was briefed that 3 of my team members were going to be laid off. I was told the morning it was going to happen and the process. You may have to deliver the message yourself to your employee, or like in my case, HR was going to be on the site, and they would give the news and explain the severance package.

I was instructed of things I should not say, not to dramatize, or offer to many explanations if they have any questions, just try to give the same answer that it was not performance-related. I was supposed to say that it was a decision made because their position becomes obsolete, and they have to layoff employees that are less time in the company.

On your first layoff, you fill the tension in the air. The plan is for the employee to arrive in the morning, ask him or her to go to a meeting room where usually is the HR representative, the manager of the employee, and the director of the site. It is good to have several people in the meeting room. It will prevent complicated situations, heated situations. Always avoid having things on the table that can be thrown as well. Be prepared to hear insults or people crying. Just try to be supportive. It helps if the company package offered is excellent. My director at the time asked for all doors to be locked to avoid repercussions, and they remain closed for three days.

After the employee is given the news, you have to accompany him or her to clean his or her desk. You usually are not allowed to go into the company computer to copy personal files. You should follow company policies and then request IT to retrieve those files to the employee.

WRAPPING UP

Once more, it was a pleasure writing this book, and once more, thank you for choosing it. I hope you enjoy it and it helps you to be a better leader. Leave the boss style in the past. People are looking for leaders who inspire them, not boss them around.

You can find me on my LinkedIn page https://www.linkedin.com/in/daniel-dias-uyourp/.

Be free to contact me at uyourp@gmail.com or go to my website www.uyourp.com if you want more information or have any questions.

www.ingramcontent.com/pod-product-compliance
Lightning Source LLC
Chambersburg PA
CBHW050000230526
45465CB00003BB/1183